Introducing Rushcraft

Introducing Rushcraft

K. Whitbourn

photographs by P. R. Whitbourn, FRIBA, ARPS

B. T. Batsford Limited

© K. Whitbourn 1969

First published 1969

Printed and bound in Great Britain by
Jarrold and Sons Limited, London and Norwich
for the publishers
B. T. BATSFORD LIMITED
4 Fitzhardinge Street, London W.1

7134 2421 4

CONTENTS

ACKNOWLEDGMENT

There are many people to whom I should like to express grateful thanks for the help they have given me in my craft, but to the following I am glad to acknowledge a particular debt in connection with the preparation of this book:

Lieutenant Commander and Mrs B. H. Charlton, for their help and encouragement in experimenting with new techniques and new materials; Mrs P. G. Burby, for her constant interest and her trouble in collecting and sending unusual specimens of basketry from different parts of the world; Miss L. Sykes, for working the embroidered bands for the sandals and the woven rush matting against which they are photographed; Miss V. Duthoit, for her help with the final tracings of the diagrams; Mrs J. Betts, for help with lampshades; Mrs P. R. Whitbourn, for making the papier-mâché chicken for the Easter table decoration; Miss C. J. Whitbourn, for typing the manuscript.

K. W.
Beverley 1969

INTRODUCTION

RUSHES AND THEIR PREPARATION

The rush most commonly used in rushcraft is *Scirpus lacustris*. This may be bought in bolts from Tom Metcalfe Arnold, Holywell, St Ives, Huntingdon, or from Dryad Handicrafts Ltd, Northgate, Leicester. Dryad Handicrafts also sell them by the pound. Apart from these rushes, it is possible to use many other leaves—iris, montbretia, grass and even carnation leaves and bean pods—in a similar way. It is, however, more difficult to get a neat effect, so the beginner is advised to use rushes at first.

The most satisfactory way of preparing the rushes (or leaves) is to lay them out of doors and water them from a watering can, turning them over so that they are all damped. If this is not possible, damp them by dropping them in water for one to two minutes. Roll them together in a piece of sacking or an old sheet and leave them all night to get pliable. Avoid getting them waterlogged, because this will cause them to shrink. Before using the rushes, wipe each one with a damp rag from tip to butt and remove any weak tips.

TOOLS

Few tools are required for rushcraft, and many of those used are ordinary household articles. The basic tools are as follows:

sharp scissors
ruler
football lacing awl
a variety of wooden moulds
clean rags
sailmaker's needle ⎫
seaming string ⎬ for plaited and
sailor's palm ⎭ stitched work

GENERAL NOTES ON FINISHING

Before embarking on a detailed description of how to make individual articles, it may be helpful to add a few general notes which will apply to all or most of the articles described:

(i) The selection of rushes is extremely important. They should be matching in thickness, and any that are spotty or unsound should be rejected.

(ii) The rows of weaving and the top of a basket must be absolutely straight.

(iii) All joins in weaving and in borders should be invisible and the weaving close and firm. To ensure a good shape it is advisable to leave an article on the mould until it is thoroughly dry.

(iv) The use of too many patterns in the same basket is not likely to give a very pleasing effect, and attention should be paid to the proportion of patterned and plain weaves. The weave used in the basket should be taken into account in choosing the handle.

DINNER MATS AND BASIC BASKETS

Round dinner mat

Materials

10 rushes $\frac{1}{2}$ in. in diameter and 16 in. in length for stakes
10 rushes $\frac{1}{4}$ in. in diameter and full length for pairing weave

Method

Arrange the thick stakes as in diagram i.

This is called CHECK WEAVE or SINGLEWEAVE (under one and over one with flattened rushes). Continue in pairing weave.

PAIRING WEAVE. Bend a fine rush in half and loop it behind the first stake, thus making a pair of weavers A and B.

Pass the weaver A over B in front of the first stake and behind the second stake.

Pass the weaver B over A and in front of the second stake and behind the third stake. Continue, using the weavers alternately, until two rounds are completed. When the weavers become short, add another thin end of rush without letting the end show, and work double for two or three strokes. Move the stakes until they are evenly spaced, and continue in pairing weave until the mat is 7 or 8 in. in diameter. Thread the weaving ends

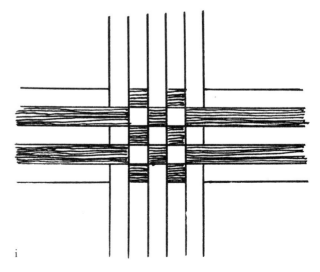

i

through the awl and draw them down through four rounds of pairing weave. Damp the stakes.

BORDER 1 Push the eye of the awl up through the last four rounds of pairing weave and thread the next stake through it. Draw the stake down under the four rounds of pairing.

Continue in this way and when the mat is perfectly round all ends may be trimmed quite close, making the mat reversible.

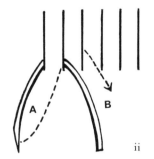

ii

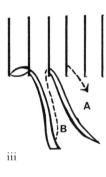

iii

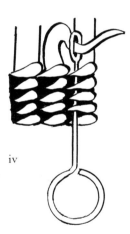

iv

1–8 Check weave

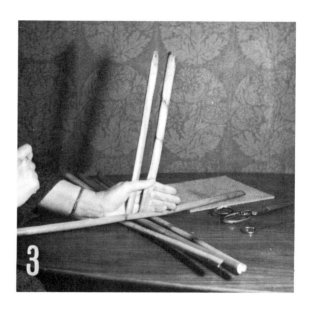

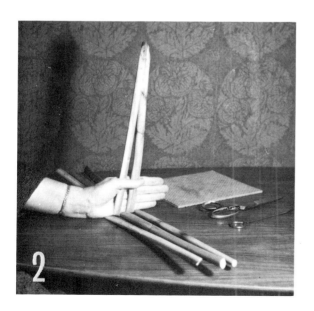

9–13 Pairing weave

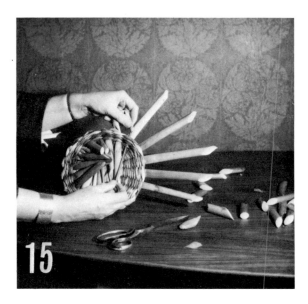

14–16 Border 1

17–18 Completed mat (both sides)

Oval dish mat

Materials

5 rushes $\frac{1}{2}$ in. in diameter and 18 in.
in length
9 rushes $\frac{1}{2}$ in. in diameter and 16 in. } stakes
in length

About 20 rushes $\frac{1}{4}$ in. in diameter and full
length for pairing weave

Method

This mat is made in the same way as the Round
Dinner Mat except that four extra stakes are
added to the five woven across in the check
weave. Fourteen rushes are therefore required, and used five by nine. Damp the stakes
before finishing with Border 2.

BORDER 2 Push the eye of the awl up through
the last four rounds of pairing weave, take
the second stake on the left behind the first,
thread it through the eye of the awl and draw
it down under the four rounds of pairing
weave.

Thread the last stake through the border
before drawing it down. When the mat is a
good shape the ends may be trimmed close
as for the Round Dinner Mat.

Two larger mats ($7'' \times 11''$ and $9'' \times 13''$ for the
check weave start) make a useful set of dish
mats.

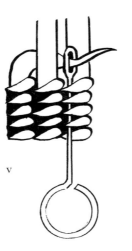

v

Square dinner mat

Materials

18 rushes $\frac{1}{2}$ in. in diameter and 20 in. in length, for stakes

About 24 rushes $\frac{1}{4}$ in. in diameter and full length for pairing weave

Method

Work as for the Round Dinner Mat until two rounds of pairing weave have been completed. In the third round, insert an extra stake by holding the corner weaver down, bending the extra stake in half, slipping it over the left-hand weaver and putting it into the corner.

Continue in pairing weave, adding one double stake in each corner. In the next round each new stake should be pressed into a right angle, making seven stakes along each side of the mat. Work two plain rounds and then add extra stakes in the corners as before. Continue in this way until the mat is the desired size. Damp the stakes.

BORDER 3 Push the eye of the awl up through the last four rounds of pairing weave, take the third stake on the left in front of the second and behind the first, thread it through the eye of the awl and draw it down under the four rounds of pairing weave.

Continue round the mat, taking care to keep the corners square, and keeping the pattern consistent by threading the last stakes through the border before drawing them down. When the mat is a good shape, the ends may be trimmed close.

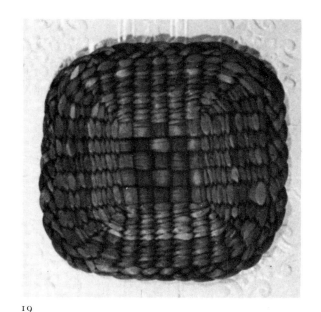

19

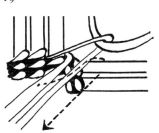

vi

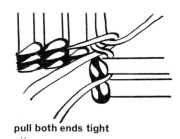

pull both ends tight

vii

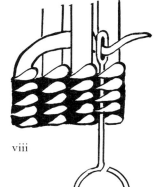

viii

20

Waste paper basket with round base

Materials

An earthenware flower pot 5 in. across base, marked with a ring 2 in. from the top and another 2 in. from the bottom
20 rushes ½ in. in diameter and 40 in. in length, for stakes
12 rushes ½ in. in diameter and full length for check weave on the sides
Finer rushes for pairing weave

Method

Start as for the Round Dinner Mat but using twenty rushes instead of ten, so that each stake is double. Exactly the same size check weave centre will be achieved, but it will be thicker and stronger. Work two rounds of tight pairing weave. In the next round work the corner stakes singly, and in each subsequent round separate more stakes, until by the time the mat is large enough to fit the base of the flower pot all stakes are single.

Tie the base on to the flower pot with soft string and make a simple FOOT-TRACK by taking each stake over the next one to the right and back into place, ready for weaving the sides of the basket.

Work 2 in. of pairing weave up the sides, then add another stake (to make an odd number for check weave) by drawing it down under four rounds of pairing weave with the awl. Using single thick rushes, change to check weave (under one and over one) starting with the thick or butt end of the rush. As soon as the weaver becomes too thin to make good checks, add another butt, overlapping it 4 or 5 in. with the first. Continue in check weave until the basket is 2 in. from the top of the flower pot, then add another weaving rush and work to the top in pairing weave. Finish the ends of the weavers by drawing

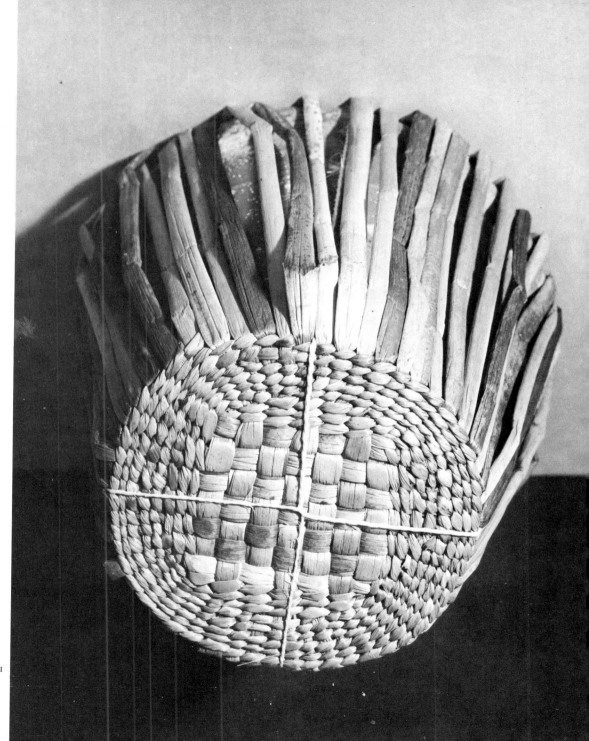

21

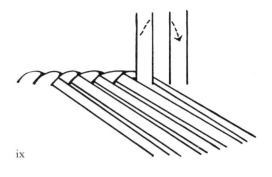

ix

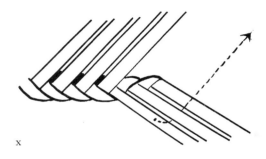

x

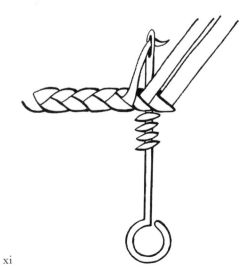

xi

them with the awl under four rounds of pairing weave.

BORDER 4 The Double Plait. The stakes should be damped before starting the border, which consists of three simple rounds:

(i) Pass each stake behind its neighbour to the right and press the end downwards against the side of the basket.

(ii) Pass each stake under its neighbour to the right, and up above the border at an angle of $45°$.

(iii) With the awl, thread each stake down behind its neighbour to the right and under four rounds of pairing weave.

Trim the ends close and leave the waste paper basket to dry thoroughly on the flower pot.

Bucket bag

Materials

An earthenware flower pot (base 7 in. in diameter) marked with a ring 2 in. from the top and another 2 in. from the bottom

28 rushes $\frac{1}{2}$ in. in diameter and 40 in. in length, for stakes

About 12 rushes $\frac{1}{2}$ in. in diameter and full length for check weave

Fine rushes for pairing weave

Method

Work in the same way as the Waste Paper Basket with Round Base except that the check weave start will be $7'' \times 7''$ double rushes instead of $5'' \times 5''$, giving a larger basket. On the sides of the basket a three rod wale may be introduced when changing from pairing weave to check weave and vice versa. For this a third weaving rush must be added.

THREE ROD WALE Take A over B and C in front of two stakes and behind one stake.

22

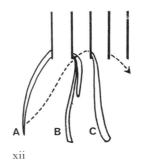

xii   xiii

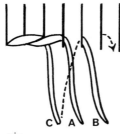

xiv

Take B (and tip of C) over C and A and in front of two stakes and behind one stake.

Take C over A and B and in front of two stakes and behind one.

To complete the round without showing the join reverse the order (CBA instead of ABC) when only one stake remains unused.

When changing to check weave, for which only one thick weaver is required, the ends of the other two should be threaded under four rounds of weaving with the awl, and trimmed. When changing to check weave, for which only two weavers are required, the third should be finished by turning upwards to make a double stake, and the pairing woven over it. Finish with Border 4.

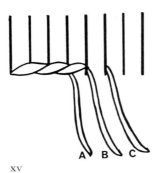

xv

ROPE HANDLES Take four long, pliable rushes for each handle. Mark the top of the basket in sixths. Using the awl, thread the four rushes (two butts and two tips) through the basket at a point $\frac{1}{2}$ in. below the border under one of the marks, and pull through till the lengths are even, i.e., half way.

Turn the basket with the open top towards you, pick up one group of rushes in the right hand and, twisting them to the right, place them in the left hand. Pick up the other group in the right hand and again twist them to the right. Lift them over the first group to the left, and continue in this way until the handle is the desired length.

Finish the handle at the next mark by placing the left-hand group inside and the right-hand group outside the basket and threading them in opposite directions through the same hole. Using the awl, weave the ends away invisibly below the border. Make another identical handle on the opposite side of the basket.

xvi

Work basket with spider base

Materials

BASKET

A round cake tin or saucepan
7 rushes $\frac{3}{8}$ in. in diameter and 24 in. in length
21 rushes $\frac{3}{8}$ in. in diameter and 12 in. in length }stakes
Fine rushes for pairing weave

LID

7 rushes $\frac{3}{8}$ in. in diameter and 20 in. in length
21 rushes $\frac{3}{8}$ in. in diameter and 10 in. in length }stakes
Fine rushes for pairing weave

23

Method

With soft string, tie the seven 24 in. rushes tightly together in the middle and trim the string. Take trouble in bending the stakes (like hairpins) over the string to give fourteen radials in proper order.

With a fine, pliable rush, work in pairing weave for one inch. Add seven stakes by drawing them down alternate stakes under four rounds of pairing. After each inch of pairing add seven more stakes in this way until the base is exactly the size of the mould. Tie it on to the mould and make a foot-track with the stakes in the same way as for the Bucket Bag, but taking each stroke over two stakes instead of one.

Turn the stakes up the sides and work 4 or 5 in. of close pairing weave. Finish with Border 1 and allow to dry on the mould.

LID Start as for the base, and when large enough tie it over the base and, without making a foot-track, work on in pairing weave up the sides for about one inch. Finish with Border 2 and leave to dry.

xvii

25

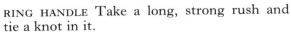

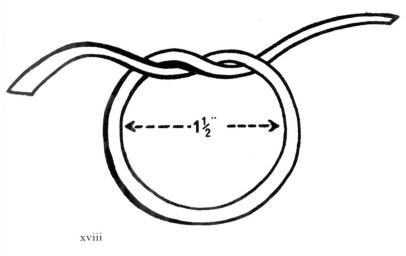

RING HANDLE Take a long, strong rush and tie a knot in it.

Wind the ends round the ring several times in opposite directions, and when they meet take them together and, twisting them to the right, wrap the ring tightly until it is closely covered. At about one inch from the finish of the wrapping add a loop of string to take the end back through the wrapping and make a neat finish.

Attach the ring to the centre of the lid with a rope made with two fine rushes.

xviii

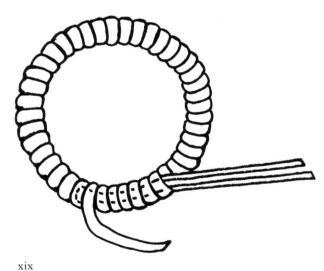

xix

Rectangular basket with lid

Materials

Wooden block $13'' \times 8\frac{1}{2}'' \times 4''$

Using the side $13'' \times 4''$ for the base, mark the sides $1\frac{1}{2}$ in. from the bottom and $1\frac{1}{2}$ in. from the top. Mark the top of the block in thirds for handle positions.

BASKET

10 or 12 rushes $\frac{1}{2}$ in. in diameter and 46 in. in length ⎫
30 rushes $\frac{1}{2}$ in. in diameter and 36 in. in length ⎬ stakes
12 rushes $\frac{1}{2}$ in. in diameter and full length for check weave
Finer rushes ($\frac{1}{4}$ in. in diameter and full length) for pairing weave

LID

6 rushes $\frac{1}{2}$ in. in diameter and 26 in. in length ⎫
26 rushes $\frac{1}{2}$ in. in diameter and 18 in. in length ⎬ stakes
7 extra stakes 12 in. in length
12 corner stakes 14 in. in length
Finer rushes for pairing weave

Method

Lay the 46 in. rushes close to each other across the table with butt and tip alternating. Working the base flat on the table, measure 17 in. from the left and place the wooden block over the stakes to the left of the mark (to hold the stakes in place while working the base). Turn up alternate stakes over the block and lay one of the 36 in. rushes across the others at right angles and work in check weave. Continue with the other 36 in. rushes until the check weave base measures $13'' \times 4''$ and with soft string tie it on to the block, leaving the stakes free and turning them up the sides.

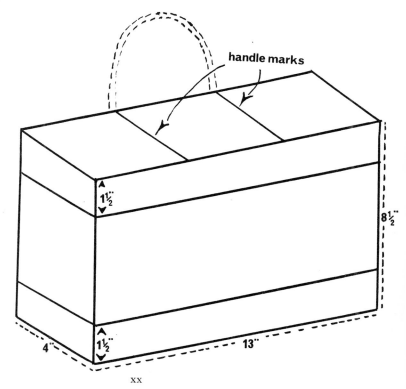

handle marks

$1\frac{1}{2}''$

$8\frac{1}{2}''$

$1\frac{1}{2}''$

$4''$

$13''$

xx

27

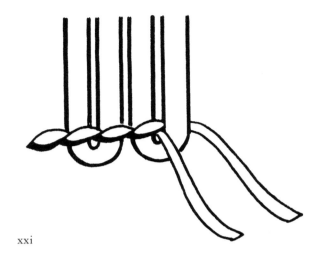

xxi

Starting on the short side work 1½ in. of pairing weave, finishing on the guide line. Add a round of three rod wale and change to check weave after adding an extra stake to make an odd number of stakes. Continue in check weave to the next guide line.

Change to three rod wale for one round, and then work in pairing weave to the top of the block exactly. Finish with Border 1.

LID Lay the six 26 in. rushes across the table and make a check weave start as for the base, and when it measures 11½″ × 2½″ work two rounds of pairing weave. Continuing to work on the table, add corner stakes (as for Square Dinner Mat) and work two more rounds of pairing weave. In the next round add four more corner stakes, and work two more rounds of pairing weave finishing just before the first handle mark at the front of the basket.

Make the slit for the handle to pass through by threading ten stakes under the six rounds of pairing weave (as for Border 1) between and outside the handle marks on the block. Thread down three stakes at the back of the lid at each of the handle marks to make holes for the hinge handle at the back of the basket. Turn the lid upside down and, picking up the pairing rushes, twist them and work in pairing weave round the end of the basket as far as the first handle hole at the back.

Turn the lid to the right side and, twisting the rushes, work back to the slit in pairing weave. Add five new stakes (to complete the slit) by bending them in half and working over both halves close to the bend.

Leave the work at this stage and, taking a new rush, work in pairing weave round the other end of the basket as far as the other hole at the back. Turn the lid on to the wrong side, and twisting the rushes, work back in pairing weave as far as the new stakes and finish by

twisting the rushes again and threading the weavers under four rounds of pairing weave.

Pick up the weaving rushes containing the new stakes and continue in pairing weave as far as the nearest handle hole. Add one new bent stake as in diagram xxi, and a third by drawing an 8 in. stake under the pairing on the stake to the right of the hole.

Leave the work at this stage and, taking a new rush, work in pairing weave across the stakes between the holes for the hinge handle, and turn the lid to the wrong side. Twist the rushes and work back in pairing weave, then twist them again and thread them under four rounds of pairing weave. Turn the lid to the right side. Pick up the weaving rushes containing the three new stakes and work across the stakes between the two holes. Add three new stakes as before, and continue in pairing weave.

Tie the lid on to the block and, continuing in pairing weave, add the last four corner stakes and work as many rounds as will give a pleasing appearance and a good fit to the lid (usually about six). Finish with Border 2.

Allow the basket and lid to dry on the block, and when both are thoroughly dry add rope handles, threading the back handle through the holes in the lid before finishing it off.

OPENWORK BASKETS

Openwork baskets are decorative and quickly made.

Openwork basket 1

Materials

A wooden block $13'' \times 8\frac{1}{2}'' \times 4''$

Using the side $13'' \times 4''$ for the base, mark the sides of the block in clear lines at 2 in. intervals, leaving $\frac{1}{2}$ in. at the top.

10 (or 12) rushes $\frac{1}{2}$ in. in diameter and 46 in. in length ⎫
About 30 rushes $\frac{1}{2}$ in. in diameter and 38 in. in length ⎬ stakes ⎭

Finer rushes ($\frac{1}{4}$ in. in diameter) for pairing weave

Method

Lay the 46 in. rushes close to each other across the table, alternating butt and tip. Measuring from the left, mark off 17 in. and, placing the wooden block left of the mark, turn back alternate rushes over the block. Work the 38 in. rushes across in check weave until the woven base is exactly the same size as that of the basket block. Tie it on to the block with string as if tying a parcel, taking care to leave the stakes free and turning them up to make the sides of the basket.

Starting on the short side, work one round of firm pairing, weaving over the beginning of the round as shown in diagrams xxii–xxiv.

Using the first 2 in. guide line, work another firm round of pairing weave and finish as before. Repeat this on the line 4 in. up the side and on the line 6 in. up the side. On the next line cross the stakes before starting the pairing weave, and continue in straight pairing weave to the top of the block. Finish with Border 1.

Mark the top of the basket in thirds, and make rope handles as for the Bucket Bag.

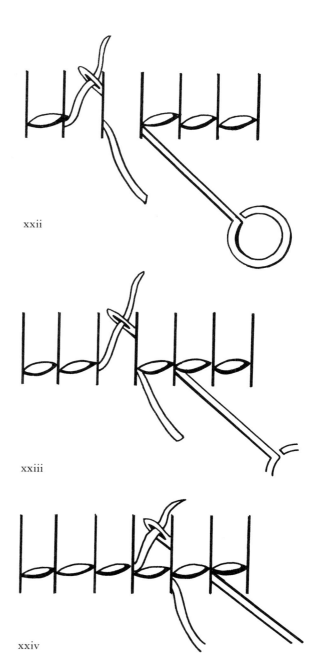

xxii

xxiii

xxiv

31

Openwork basket 2

Materials

The same wooden block as for Openwork Basket 1, using the side $8\frac{1}{2}'' \times 4''$ for the base
10 or 12 rushes $\frac{1}{2}$ in. in diameter and 48 in. in length ⎫
20 to 24 rushes $\frac{1}{2}$ in. in diameter and 44 in. in length ⎬ stakes
Finer rushes ($\frac{1}{4}$ in. in diameter) for pairing weave

Method

Leaving an inch at the top, draw four lines round the block at intervals of $2\frac{2}{5}$ in. and work as for Openwork Basket 1.

When the border is finished, remove the basket from the block and bend the ends inward as shown in diagram xxv.

Holding the folds in position, place the top inch of pairing weave under a heavy object such as a sewing machine and leave for twelve hours. Put on rope handles and a button and loop.

BUTTON IN HALF HITCH (NEEDLE HITCHING) Take a fine rush, thread it through the eye of a rug needle and, tying a knot in it, work into the ring a series of half hitches.

Cover the second end as well as the ring. In the second and subsequent rounds work into the loops (twice into some of them) until the button cover is about $1\frac{1}{2}$ in. in diameter. Fill it with rushes or a button mould and work the back neatly. Sew the button to the front of the basket with soft string.

On the back of the basket mark two points $\frac{1}{2}$ in. each side of the centre at a distance of $\frac{1}{2}$ in. from the top. Using the awl, thread two rushes (one butt and one tip) through the basket at one of these points and pull them through till the ends are even in length.

xxv

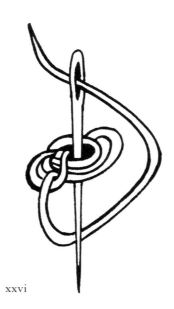

xxvi

Twist the rushes together as if making a rope handle. When the loop is large enough to take the button easily, finish by placing the left-hand coil inside and the right-hand coil outside the basket at the second mark, and thread them through the same hole in opposite directions. Using the awl, weave the ends away invisibly.

Openwork basket 3

Materials

As for Openwork Basket 1, but with more fine rushes for pairing weave

Method

Mark the sides of the block as shown in diagram xxvii.

Using the 13″ × 4″ side of the block as the base, work a check weave base as for Openwork Basket 1, but making sure that the total number of stakes is divisible by four.

Tie the base on to the block and work the first 1½ in. in pairing weave, weaving the ends away under the last four rounds. Cross every second stake over three (i.e., stake/space/stake each time) at the beginning of the centre block of pairing weave (see photograph 26); then cross them back again at the beginning of the top inch of pairing weave.

Finish with Border 4 and rope handles.

Openwork basket 4

Materials

As for Openwork Basket 1, but with extra rushes for pairing weave

Method

Mark the sides of the block as shown in diagram xxviii.

Using the 13″ × 4″ side of the block as the base, work a check weave base as for Openwork Basket 1, but making sure that the total number of stakes is divisible by four.

Tie the base on to the block and work three rounds of pairing weave. *Cross alternate stakes as for Openwork Basket 3, working three rounds of pairing weave before crossing them back into place**. Repeat from * to ** and continue to the top of the basket in pairing weave.

Finish with Border 4 and rope handles.

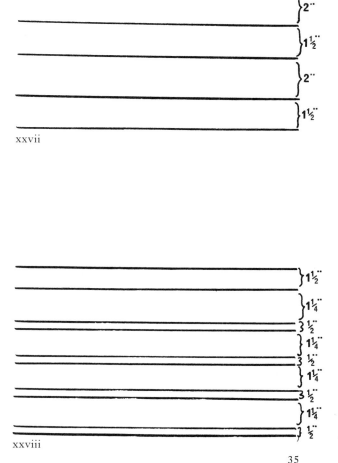

xxvii

xxviii

35

27

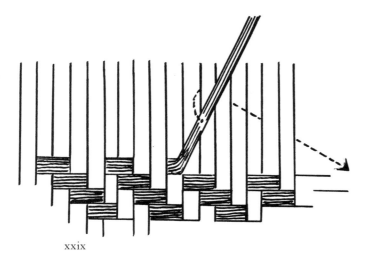

xxix

PATTERNED WEAVES

Square waste paper basket in twill weave

Materials

A wooden block with base 5″ × 5″, top 7″ × 7″ and height about 8 in.

24 rushes ½ in. in diameter and 38 in. in length, for stakes

About 12 rushes ½ in. in diameter and full length, for twill weave

A few fine rushes for pairing weave

Method

Lay ten rushes close together across the base and weave another ten into them in check weave, covering the base. Turn the rushes up for the sides of the basket and tie the base on to the block with string.

Start pairing weave in the middle of one side using two rushes, one of which should be a butt. Leave enough of the butt end to make an extra stake (an odd number is necessary for twill weave) and use the rest of the rush for pairing weave, taking the tip of the looped second rush with it for the first few strokes. Work three rounds of pairing weave, and in the third round introduce an extra 38 in. rush in each corner (as in the Square Dinner Mat). Take a thick butt and start TWILL WEAVE under two and over two stakes.

Continue in twill weave to within ½ in. of the top, then work three or four rounds of pairing weave.

Finish with Border 4 and leave on the block to dry.

Basket in diagonal weave

Materials

A wooden block 9 in. high with oval base
17″ × 3½″
40 rushes ½ in. in diameter and 36 in.
in length
12 rushes ½ in. in diameter and 46 in. } stakes
in length
Rushes ⅜ in. in diameter and full length, for
patterned weave

Method

Measure the base and subtract breadth from
length (13½ in.). Draw a thick line this length
on a piece of cardboard. Take a 36 in. stake
and lay it across the line so that the centre of
the stake lies on the line. Place another
beside it (butt and tip alternating) with edges
touching, and continue until the line is
covered. Take two 46 in. rushes and work in
pairing weave along the line over two and
under two stakes, leaving 14 in. before
starting, to make two extra stakes. When the
row of pairing is finished there should be
enough length to make two extra stakes at the
other end. Take two more 46 in. stakes and,
immediately above the middle line, work a
row of REVERSE PAIRING WEAVE under two and
over two, leaving 14 in. for end stakes as
before.

This makes a row of long chain pairing down
the centre of the base. Take two strong thick
weaving rushes and, leaving the same length
for stakes, start pairing over one and under
one at the same point as in the first row. On
reaching the opposite end of the base, lay
aside the weavers, take two new ones and,
leaving 14 in. of them for stakes, work under
one and over one in reverse pairing weave
round the end stakes and along the sides.
On completing the round pick up the first

28

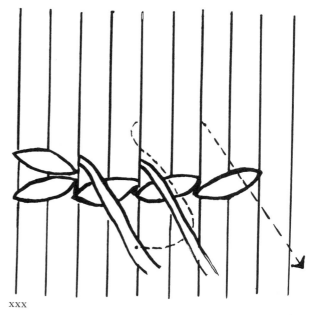

xxx

37

29

xxxi

set of weavers and work a round in pairing weave. Using the two sets of weavers alternately and adding extra stakes at the ends as necessary, continue until the base is exactly the size of the block. Tie on to the block.

Make a FOUR ROD WALE using the same method as for the three rod wale (see Bucket Bag) but going over three stakes and under one. Work over a core of rush, using two strong rushes for the core. At the end of the round weave one end away under the pairing weave base and, turning the stakes up the sides of the block, work three rounds of three rod wale. Count the stakes, making sure the number is divisible by four, and then add one extra. Draw one of the three weavers down under the wale and continue with two. With one weaver pair over one and under three; with the other, pair over three and under one. Continue in this way to within an inch of the top of the basket, then work three rounds of three rod wale.

BORDER 5 Push the eye of the awl up through the three rounds of three rod wale, take the second stake on the left in front of the first, thread it through the eye of the awl and draw it down under the three rounds of three rod wale.

Pull tight. When the top of the basket is level, trim the ends of the rushes.

The handles of the basket illustrated are made with a tight three-plait approximately $\frac{3}{4}$ in. wide (see section on plaiting, page 39), but it could be finished with rope handles.

SECTION II
Plaits

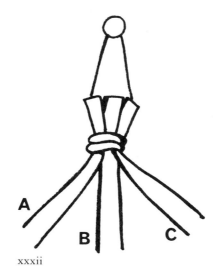

xxxii

As well as the weaves described in the previous section, it is possible to make many attractive articles (dinner mats, floor mats, fruit bowls, etc.) by plaiting the rushes. The simple three-plait can be used in many different ways, the thickness of the plait being varied according to the size of the article. As an alternative to rope handles the round and square plaits are excellent—strong and comfortable to hold—and the flat plaits or braids may also be used for basket handles.

Simple three-plait

Tie three $\frac{1}{2}$ in. butts together firmly and fasten the string round a hook in the wall. Use the right hand only for plaiting, keeping the rushes in place under the left thumb.

Pass A across B to the right in a short stroke at an angle of $45°$. Pass C across A to the left in a short stroke at an angle of $45°$. Pass B across C to the right in a short stroke at an angle of $45°$.

Continue in this way until the desired length is achieved, keeping the plait the same thickness throughout by adding another butt as each rush becomes too thin. Add the new butt in the middle of the plait, leaving the ends on the back and trimming close when the plait is dry. When two yards of plait have been made, loop it up to the hook again.

xxxiii

30

Plaited dinner mat

Materials
About 24 rushes $\frac{1}{2}$ in. in diameter and full length
A sailmaker's needle
3-ply seaming string

Method
To make a neat start, take three matching rushes and, laying two together, double the third over them as shown in diagram xxxiv.

Fasten them to a hook in the wall and plait as described above, joining new rushes by slipping the butts between the two strands which make up each group of the plait. There will then be no ends to trim.

When some five yards of plait have been completed, coil the beginning (keeping the plait face to face and with the edge flat on the table) and stitch firmly. Continue to attach the plait to the coiled centre by stitching through the loose plait and through the last round of the coil with STAB STITCH (working through the centre of the plaits so that no string is visible).

To join a new length of string, use a reef knot, trim the ends neatly and pull the stitch tight so that the knot disappears into the plait. To finish, trim one rush from each group and, using the awl, weave the remaining ends into the preceding round, in pattern. Stitch securely.

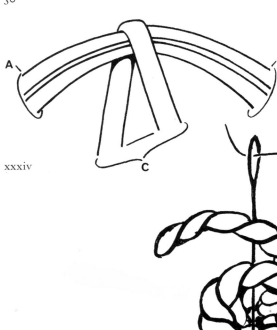

A

B

C

xxxiv

xxxv

40

Floor mat

Materials

About 50 yards of three-plait, $\frac{3}{4}$ in. in width.

For this, use four or five rushes in each group, plaiting with the right hand only and twisting each group to the right as a stroke is made. A curtain ring may be carried down the plait to ensure a uniform width.

A sailmaker's needle and sailor's palm

3-ply seaming string

Method

Take 48 in. of three-plait, bind each end tightly and trim close to the binding. Place a marker 24 in. along the plait. Using the plait face to face (and not edge to edge) coil one end round tightly two or three times and stitch firmly. Coil flat on the table and stab stitch as for the Plaited Dinner Mat. Continue until the half-way mark is reached. Start at the other end and, coiling in the opposite direction (like a letter S), work to the marker and stitch firmly to the first half of the scroll. Make two more scrolls in the same way. Join the scrolls together, keeping them in a straight line.

Bind the end of the remaining length of plait and trim close, then stitch it in a straight line round the scrolls, blind-stitching across the spaces. Coil and stitch the remaining length of plait and finish as for the Plaited Dinner Mat.

Log basket

Materials

50 to 60 yards of three-plait 2 in. in width
(9 or 10 lb of rushes will be required)
A sailmaker's needle and sailor's palm
3-ply seaming string

Method

Bind one end of the plait and coil it anti-clockwise, face to face. Stab stitch, keeping the edge of the plait on the table to achieve a flat base. Continue until the base measures 18 in. in diameter.

Raise the plait and stitch it flat on top of the last two rounds of the base to start the sides. Continue, keeping the sides perpendicular, until the sides measure 18 in. Taper the plait and finish by weaving the ends into the plait of the round below with the awl. Stitch securely.

Mark the position of the handles with chalk, placing them so as to conceal the bulge made when changing from base to sides. Take a sufficient length of plait to go twice across the base, twice up the sides and project above the top of the basket to make comfortable handles. Bind each end, trim close, abut the ends and stitch them together across the bindings. Join a second identical length of plait in the same way, pin both in position with the joins underneath the basket, and stitch securely. The projecting handles may be damped and wrapped tightly with twisted rushes or a fine plait.

32

33

Plaited bowl

Materials
6 yards of three-plait, about $\frac{3}{4}$ in. in width
A sailmaker's needle
3-ply seaming string

Method
Start the base as for the Log Basket and when it is 7 or 8 in. in diameter put in a marker and raise the plait $\frac{3}{8}$ in. for the next round. Working on the outside of the basket, make three or four rounds, raising the plait $\frac{3}{8}$ in. each time. When the shape is pleasing, continue the sides straight (as for the Log Basket) until the desired height is reached. Taper the plait and weave the ends into the round below with the awl, finishing at a point above the marker.

To finish the top, cut a strong piece of willow or hazel long enough to go round the top and overlap 3 or 4 in. SLYPE the ends (i.e., taper the last 4 in. of each end so that they fit neatly together) and join them with Sellotape. Place this ring on top of the basket along with two thick rushes, and insert four good rushes through the basket below the last round of plait. Thread the rug needle with the first of the four rushes and stitch over the willow and under the first round of plaiting just ahead of the fourth rush.

Continue in this way with each rush in turn until the willow is completely covered.

Round plait

Take two thick rushes, double one over the other and tie to a hook in the wall so that the work can be done downwards at tension (diagram xxxvi). Take two ends in each hand and bring the outside rush on the right round the back of the plait and between the two rushes on the left and back to the right (diagram xxxvii). Take the outside rush on the left round the back of the plait and between the rushes on the right and back to the left (diagram xxxviii). Continue in this way to the desired length.

A thicker plait may be made in a similar way but starting with three rushes. Double two over the first and, with three ends in each hand, take the outside rush on the right under the plait, over one rush on the left and back to the right again. Take the outside rush on the left under the plait, over one rush on the right and back to the left. Continue in the same way. These plaits may also be worked over a core of rush or other material.

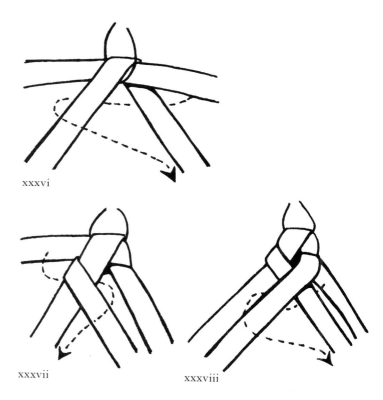

xxxvi

xxxvii

xxxviii

Square plait

Take four good rushes, double them over a piece of string and tie them to a hook in the wall. Take four ends in each hand, bring the outside one on the right under the plait, up between the four rushes (two and two) on the left and over two back to the right.

Bring the outside rush on the left under the plait, up between the four rushes on the right and over two back to the left. Continue in the same way to the desired length.

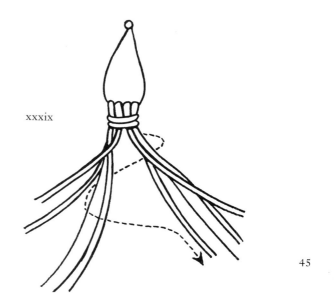

xxxix

45

34

Flat five-plait

Tie together five even rushes by the butt. Spread them out flat over the left hand and plait with the right hand, bringing the right-hand rush over, under and over the middle three rushes; with the left hand, turn the left-hand rush over the weaving rush and hold it under the left thumb. Start again at the right-hand edge and, turning the outside rush, weave it over, under and over the middle three as before. The weaving rush should be taken across at an angle of 45°, and care taken to fold over the edge rush on each side neatly.

Seven, nine or any number of rushes may be used in this way to make a wider plait. The handles of the basket shown below are made with a flat five-plait and spliced underneath.

THE SPLICE It is a good plan to practise this on a short piece of plait (about 12 in. long) before using it on a basket. Bringing the ends round to meet each other, place the two diagonal weavers together and, with the awl, weave away the ends in pattern. When the join is sufficiently strong, the ends may be trimmed close. If done carefully, this join will not show at all.

When using this plait for the handles of a large basket use double rushes, cutting off the underneath rush before splicing to keep the splice neat. For the basket illustrated above 70 in. of plait was used. The splice should be placed underneath the basket.

Grecian plait

Tie together five rushes as for the Flat Five-Plait, but bring the outside rush on the right over two into the centre. Take the outside rush on the left over two into the centre of the plait and continue in this way, folding the edge carefully. This method produces a good firm plait, but for basket handles the rushes should be used double.

It is almost impossible to splice this plait invisibly. To join, whip the ends with string, trim close, abut them, and stitch firmly across the whipping.

SEATING

Traditional method

Materials

A rectangular stool frame marked with arrows
as in diagram xl
About $1\frac{1}{2}$ lb rushes

Method

Bend a rush over bar D and, taking both
ends together, work round corner AB by
stroking and twisting the two ends to the
right until they look like one rush. Lay this
tightly over bar B and, bringing it up in the
inner edge of the frame, twist with the left
hand in the opposite direction, i.e., away from
the corner, as shown by the arrows. When it is
as one rush, lay it carefully at right angles over
the coil already in position and over bar A
and bring it up through the inner edge of the
frame. This completes the first corner and
all others are done in the same way, turning the
stool in a clockwise direction.

All joins should be made with a reef knot at a
point half way along the sides until the seating
is nearly finished, when it will be necessary to
join underneath. The knots should then be
covered so that the underside is as neat as the
top.

The seating will wear better and look better
if it is well packed so, when about eight
rounds have been completed, turn the stool
upside down on a table and fill the underneath pockets with dry waste rushes, pushing

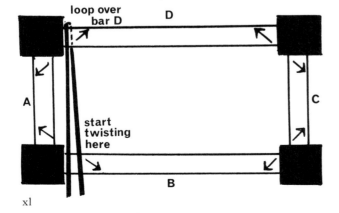

loop over bar D

D

start twisting here

A

B

C

xl

48

them well into the corners and padding until the seat is quite hard. After every six or eight rounds add more padding.

When the short sides are complete, take the coil backwards and forwards over bars B and D in a figure of eight. When the last coil is in place, turn the stool upside down and tie the rushes with a small knot (a half hitch is best) to one of the coils in the opposite section. Weave the end out of sight with the awl.

The seating should be allowed to dry after completing sections A and C and another coil inserted before going on to complete B and D. These should also be allowed to dry and a final coil inserted before finishing.

Orkney seating

Materials

A rectangular stool frame of the type illustrated on the right of photograph 35. Holes should be made in four places on the outside of the long sides, and grooves to hold the leather or twisted rush pairing are an advantage
A quantity of strong rushes. Fewer are required than for the traditional method, but they should be strong and of good appearance
About 3 yards of leather thonging

Method

Fasten a rush to one of the short bars, take it over the opposite bar and back again. Continue wrapping in this way, joining the new rush with a reef knot underneath the seat and covering the knot with the next rush, until the seat is raised above the level of the wood on the long sides. Finish with a half hitch on the underside and tuck the end away.

Prepare three pads of rushes the length of the short bars of the stool frame. Take the leather (or twisted rush) and work a row of pairing weave at each of the marked places across the wrapped seating, taking even groups of rushes each time. At the same time, insert the pads of rushes through the centre of the wrapped seat between each row of pairing weave. Finish safely and neatly.

In addition to the two examples illustrated, any of the methods commonly used for string seating may be used for rush seating.

35

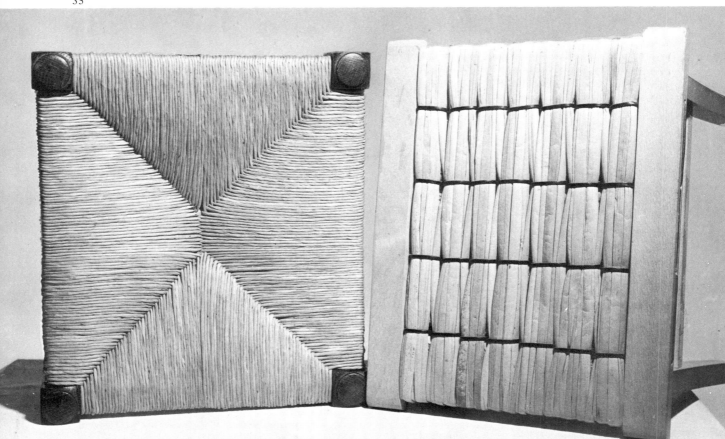

BASKETS BY THE TWISTED METHOD

Half hitch basket

Materials
About $1\frac{1}{2}$ lb strong rushes, $\frac{1}{2}$ in. in diameter
A few yards of strong brown string

Method
Take two rushes and insert between them at a point half way along, a piece of strong brown string 6 in. in length. Tie a loose knot in the part containing the string, bind the ring made by the knot with the shortest of the four ends of rush to strengthen it and, taking the remaining three rushes together, twist them in a clockwise direction. Three rushes twisted together are used throughout the basket and joins should be made by inserting the butt of the new rush between the other three and twisting firmly.
First round: make six loops into the ring at the centre of the base (the technique is similar to needle hitching, but no needle is used). In order to get them even, the loops may be measured over the first two fingers of the left hand.
Second round: make three loops into each loop of the previous round.
Third round: make two loops into each loop of the previous round.
Fourth round: plain, i.e., one loop into each loop of the previous round.
Fifth round: make two loops into every second loop of the previous round, and one into the loops between.
Sixth and *all subsequent rounds*: plain.

Finish the top of the basket over a core of strong rush (or cord) by wrapping closely with the twisted rush. Wrap handles in the same way over a core of string or cord.

36

37

38

39

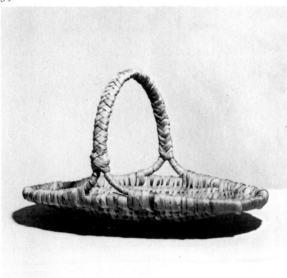

Garden trug on a willow frame

Materials
A willow or cane frame (obtainable from Dryad Handicrafts, Leicester)
About 1 lb rushes

Method
Three rushes twisted together are used throughout the basket, and joins should be made by inserting the butt of the new rush between the other three and twisting firmly.

Wrap the handle closely, starting at the left arm, working up to the V, over it and down the right arm. Leave the ends to be covered when the basket weaving is done. Turn the basket round and work the other end of the handle by wrapping the left arm of it as far as the V. Leave the coil at the V and, starting with new rushes, work up the right arm, over the double part of the handle and over the left-hand coil for two turns. Flattening the rushes from the left-hand coil, turn them back over the two turns just made with the right-hand coil and, using the right-hand coil, make two turns over the handle. Bring the flattened rushes over these two turns and on to the handle, working over them with the right-hand coil for two turns. Continue in this way across the handle to the wrapped V, and finish neatly.

To start the basket, wrap the middle 2 in. of one end of the frame, then start to weave under and over the ribs, going twice over the frame each time it is reached. Press the weaving close together to cover the ribs. When about 5 in. of weaving is done, start at the other end of the basket and, working a little at each end, aim to finish in the middle of the basket, removing the extra cane and nails when the weaving is close to them. Complete the last few rows of weaving with the awl, and weave the ends away neatly.

The smaller garden trug is made in the same way, but with single untwisted rush. The handle is covered with a square plait worked over the cane handle.

Waste paper basket in twisted rush

Materials

A flower pot 6½ in. or 7 in. across the base; 56 rushes ½ in. in diameter for stakes. The necessary length may be calculated by measuring the flower pot from the rim, down the side, across the base and up to the rim again, and adding 16 in. for the border.
½ lb finer rushes for weaving

Method

Take two of the thick rushes (butt and tip) and twist them together until they look like one rush. Do this with fourteen double rushes, lay them side by side along a working table, clamp them down at each end (to retain the twist) and leave to dry. When dry, damp the centre 6 in. and weave a corresponding number of twisted double rushes under and over them in the manner of check weave, although the twisted rush will give a quite different effect. Clamp down the ends of the new rushes to keep the twist and allow them to dry.

40

Carefully damp all the stakes and tie the base on to the bottom of the flower pot (as for Waste Paper Basket with Round Base). Three rushes twisted together are used for weaving throughout, and joins made in the same way as for the Half Hitch Basket. Work several rounds of RANDING WEAVE (i.e., under one and over one, as in check weave), leaving about 18 in. of the weaver at the beginning for use as an extra stake. Continue until the base is covered, then lay aside the weaving rush and make a foot-track exactly on the edge of the base, as for Waste Paper Basket with Round Base. Pick up the weaving rush and continue in randing weave for about 2 in. Twist three rushes together to make a second weaver, and work it above the first one under and over the same stakes (see photograph 40). Continue in this way to within 2 in. of the top. Twist the two weavers together into one, and continue in randing weave to the top.

Damp the stakes and, twisting them well, work Border 1 very tightly.

SECTION IV
Dress accessories

41

HATS

Rush hats are cool and shady for the garden or on the beach.

Coolie hat

Materials
½ lb rushes ½ in. in diameter

Method
Cut about a dozen rushes 30 in. long and, taking six of these, bend them in half over a full length rush. Leave 15 in. at the butt end of the long rush to act as a stake with the six, thus giving the odd number required for check weave. Tie the six together with the long rush and, using the long end, weave under and over in a cone shape. It is a good plan to work over a cardboard cone shaped to fit comfortably over the head. Introduce new stakes as necessary by doubling them over the weaving rush. They are best introduced between the same two rushes each time and at regular intervals.

After about twelve rounds the crown will usually be deep enough for a child's hat and the rest may be worked flat on the table, introducing more stakes as the brim gets wider. Finish with four rounds of pairing weave and Border 2.

A small plait may be threaded through each side of the crown to tie under the chin.

Openwork hat

Materials

A pudding basin large enough to fit the head
Strong rushes matching in thickness
for stakes
A few finer rushes for pairing weave
} in all ½ lb

Method

Cut twelve rushes 34 in. in length and make a check weave start in the centre. Work one round of pairing weave and add corner stakes as for the Square Dinner Mat. Work another round to get the stakes evenly spaced and tuck the ends of the weavers away under the pairing weave. Tie on to the pudding basin.

Take new weaving rushes and, crossing the stakes an inch down as for Openwork Basket 1, work two rounds of pairing weave and finish neatly. Take new weaving rushes and, crossing the stakes again, work two more rounds of pairing weave an inch further down the

42

crown and tuck the ends away neatly. Take new weaving rushes and, crossing the stakes again, work three rounds for the base of the crown.

Remove the pudding basin and work three more rounds of pairing weave flat on the table, introducing new stakes as required to give a good brim. Tuck the weaving rushes away neatly. Take new weaving rushes and, crossing the stakes an inch away from the weaving, work two rounds of pairing weave and tuck the weaving rushes away neatly.

With new weaving rushes start the edge by crossing the stakes an inch further out and weaving three or four rounds of pairing weave. Finish with Border 1 or Border 2. Whilst the brim is still damp shape it in a good sweeping line and leave to dry.

Breton sailor hat in folded figure-of-eight plait

Materials

3 oz rushes $\frac{1}{2}$ in. in diameter
3 oz rushes $\frac{1}{4}$ in. in diameter

Method

This hat is made entirely by hand with no block or mould and no needle. The rushes are used flat like ribbon, and joins made by overlapping 3 or 4 in. and working the rushes double in the overlap.

Tie a knot in one of the thicker rushes and work as shown in diagrams xli and xlii.

When the first rush has been used, join a fine rush to the working end and a thick rush to the other end and continue throughout in the same manner. Shape by hand and finish neatly.

For an adult, the hat could be made with a shallower crown and broader brim.

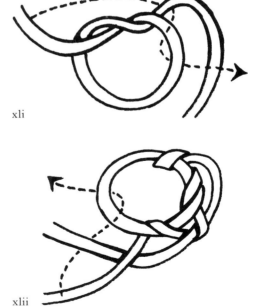

xli

xlii

Mexican hat

Materials

An earthenware flower pot large enough to
fit the head and tapering sharply to the base
A small flower pot with top exactly matching
the base of the large one in size
$\frac{1}{2}$ lb rushes matching in thickness, eight or
ten of which should be cut to 46 in. in length,
for stakes

Method

Make a check weave centre with the ten rushes (or enough to cover the base of the small flower pot). Take one of these rushes under and over the others to start check weave round the sides of the small flower pot. This leaves an uneven number as required for check weave. Continue weaving evenly to the top of the small flower pot and place it over the base of the large one. Continue in check weave, adding as many extra stakes as are required to keep the weaving neat and close, in the same way as for the Coolie Hat.

Remove the crown from the flower pots and damp the stakes. Working flat on the table, make a wide brim in check weave (at least eight rounds) adding extra stakes as required. Finish with four rounds of pairing weave and Border 1 worked from the top of the brim. Whilst the ends are still untrimmed, pull them tight to get the brim turned up all round.

SANDALS

Materials

6 or 7 yards of three-plait $\frac{3}{4}$ in. wide
A sailmaker's needle
3-ply seaming string
1 pair of insoles
1 sq. ft coloured felt

Method

First, measure the size of the foot (the sandals illustrated are ladies' size $5-5\frac{1}{2}$) and draw a line of that length on a piece of cardboard, making a mark one inch from the toe and another one inch from the heel. Whip the beginning of the plait tightly with string and trim close to the string. Using this end, and holding the work in the position shown in diagram xliii, bend back $3\frac{1}{2}$ in. (face to face) and bring the plait round the end and up again. Stab stitch through the three thicknesses of plait. Bring the loose end down to the mark one inch from the heel, stab stitching it to the previous round as far as the instep, then blind-stitching as far as the heel mark. Turn the plait up and stab stitch back to the instep.

Work two complete rounds, then a further half round at the toe end, finishing at the instep. A further round may be added if the foot is wide. Finish by tapering the plait and weaving the ends neatly into the previous round. Make another rush sole to correspond. Take the bought insoles and trim at the toes to match the rush soles. Cover them with felt (see photograph 44).

44

Mules

Attach the insoles to the rush soles with strong loop-stitch in string. Make the plaited strap by threading four rushes through the edge of the rush soles, starting at a point about $1\frac{1}{2}$ in. from the toe. Draw them through half way, making eight ends for the plait. Using the same method as for the flat five-plait, but using all eight ends, work a sufficient length to fit comfortably across the foot. Weave the ends away neatly into the rush sole on the opposite side.

Embroidered sandals

Cut four lengths of webbing to fit comfortably across the foot (those across the instep will be considerably longer than across the toe) and embroider them. Attach the insoles to the rush soles with strong loop-stitch in string, tucking the ends of the embroidered bands in between the two soles before the loop-stitching is done. A piece of strong elastic may be attached to the instep band to fit round the heel.

If desired, heel pieces may be made by coiling a further length of plait and stitching it to the rush sole.

length of foot

1"   1"

xliii

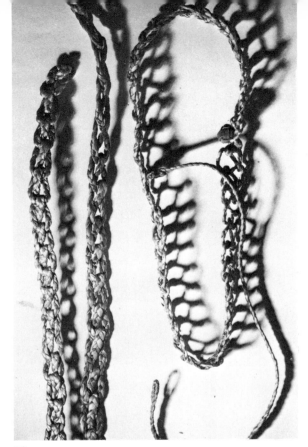

45

BELTS

Many decorative plaits may be used for belts and can be produced in any width to suit prevailing fashion. Photograph 45 shows a Drummer's Plait belt, a Double Chain Plait belt and shoestring belt made from a fine three-plait.

Drummer's plait

Work several yards of fine three-plait. Form a loop at the beginning of the plait and, putting the finger and thumb of the right hand through the loop, draw the working end of the plait through to make another loop.

Continue in this way to the required length, working downwards at tension and keeping the loops even.

Take the plait round the last loop twice to strengthen it and stitch the two thicknesses together before weaving the ends neatly away with a rug needle. Finish the other end neatly and attach a button of suitable size. The button may be covered by needle hitching as on Openwork Basket 2.

Double chain plait

Work several yards of fine three-plait. Make a loop at the beginning of the plait and, working downwards at tension, push the working end down through the loop, thus forming another loop alongside.

Take the working end down through the new loop and continue in this way, keeping the loops even. Finish as for the Drummer's Plait, by doubling the last loop, weaving away the ends and attaching a button.

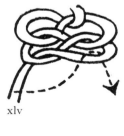

xlv

xliv

62

HANDBAGS

Shoulder bag with captive lid

Materials

A wooden block $9\frac{1}{2}'' \times 6\frac{1}{2}'' \times 2\frac{1}{2}''$

BAG

5 rushes $\frac{1}{2}$ in. in diameter and 36 in. in length ⎫
11 or 12 rushes $\frac{1}{2}$ in. in diameter and 30 in. in length ⎬ stakes
12 or more rushes $\frac{1}{2}$ in. in diameter and full length for check weave ⎭
Fine rushes for pairing weave

LID

28 rushes $\frac{1}{2}$ in. in diameter and 14 in. in length, for stakes
Fine rushes for pairing weave

HANDLE

2 yards of three-plait about 1 in. in width

Method

Using the stakes, work a check weave base for the bag, $6\frac{1}{2}'' \times 2\frac{1}{2}''$. Tie the base on to the block and turn the stakes up the sides of the block.

Work about an inch of pairing weave up the sides, then add an extra stake by drawing a butt under four rows of pairing weave with the awl. Using the thick rushes work in check weave, starting with a butt. When the rush becomes too thin to make good checks add another butt, overlapping 4 or 5 in. Continue in check weave to within an inch of the top, then work in pairing weave to the top of the block. Finish with Border 1. Leave the basket on the block and work the lid over it.

LID Lay twelve stakes (double the first and last, making fourteen in all) flat across the table and with fine rushes work in pairing

weave across the middle, keeping the end stakes double. After one row, twist the weavers together, turn the lid over and work in pairing weave back to the beginning. Twist the rushes and turn the lid back to the right side. Working always on the same side of the centre line, continue in this way for one inch of close pairing weave and in the last row separate the end stakes, taking them singly. Go back to the middle again and work another inch of close pairing weave the other side of it. On the last row separate the end stakes and use them singly. Tie the lid on to the wooden block.

Measure the handle plait carefully for a comfortable length from the shoulder and join it at the base of the bag by whipping the ends tightly with string, trimming close and sewing together end to end. Pin the handle plait in place and work the lid round it, adding two extra stakes at each end in the same way as for the Rectangular Basket with Lid. Work four to six rounds of pairing weave and finish with Border 2.

When the basket is dry stitch the plait on to it with soft string, concealing the stitches in the pattern of the plait.

SECTION V
Furnishing accessories

Many delightful baskets may be made by stitching.

HOUSEHOLD BASKETS

Ali Baba linen basket

Materials

1 bolt good rushes
About 80 yards no. 12 cane
A large rug needle

Method

Slype the end of the cane (i.e., taper it) and coil it with six rushes in an anti-clockwise direction. Thread the needle with a good pliable rush and stitch the first round of the coil closely. The stitching rush is brought over the top of the coil and through the top of the previous round. The stitches on the second round must be evenly spaced and those on all subsequent rounds should be in line with them so as to give a ribbed effect. On the base (though *not* on the sides) it will be necessary to start new ribs when the spaces between the stitches become too wide. It is advisable to keep the stitching fairly close together on the base to allow for the increase in the size of the space as the sides are built up. The stitching may be done from the inside of the basket, but the effect is better if the needle goes through the coil from the outside.

47

Joins in the coil should be made by inserting new rushes in the centre alongside the cane. Make the base about 12 in. in diameter (or larger if desired).

The sides may be shaped in any way; a pear shape is pleasing, but the one illustrated was brought out very gradually to a diameter of 20 in. and then turned fairly sharply in again to a diameter of about 12 in. A thick coil was added below the last round on the inside of the basket to support the lid.

LID Wind some odd rushes into a ball about the size of a tennis ball, and using a rather finer coil (without the cane centre) and a finer stitching rush, cover the ball neatly. When the ball is almost covered, widen the coil, introduce a cane centre and shape the lid outwards in a pleasing curve until it fits the rim of the basket. Finish neatly.

48

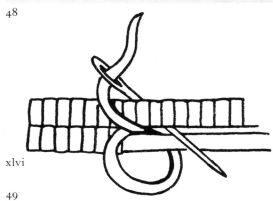

xlvi

49

Coiled basket for rolls or fruit

Materials
About ½ lb rushes depending on the size of the bowl
A rug needle

Method
Twist several rushes together to make a core rather thicker than a pencil. Thread the rug needle with a strong rush and, coiling the rush core, sew it together, covering it entirely with FIGURE-OF-EIGHT STITCH.

Continue in this way, forming the basket into a pleasing shape, and finish by tapering the coil and stitching over it into the coil below. No border is needed. This work is very slow, but the finished basket is firm and durable.

Waste paper basket in Mariposa weave

Materials
15 yards of no. 3 cane
About 1 lb rushes ½ in. in diameter

Method
Tie a knot in the middle of a strong rush. Taper the end of the cane and conceal it in the ring made by the rush knot. Using one of the rushes as a core with the cane, bind with the other rush, working into the centre ring for the first round. Introduce more rushes to make a thicker core as the work proceeds.

For MARIPOSA WEAVE, make a long stroke with the binding rush over the free end of the coil and over the coil in the previous round, bringing it up between the two coils to the right of the long stroke. Carry the binding rush across the front of the long stroke and behind the upper coil, binding the coil once before making the next long stroke.

Keep the first finger of the left hand between the coils so that the space between them is even throughout the basket.

No border is necessary, but the basket is strengthened by the addition of one round of figure-of-eight stitch worked with a needle over the last two coils.

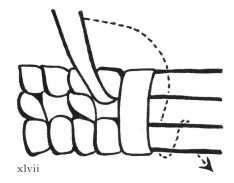

xlvii

FLOWER CONTAINERS

Check weave trough

50

Materials

A rectangular flower trough, $15'' \times 3\frac{1}{4}'' \times 4''$
6 rushes $\frac{1}{2}$ in. in diameter and 42 in. in length
28 rushes $\frac{1}{2}$ in. in diameter and 30 in. in length } stakes
6 rushes $\frac{1}{2}$ in. in diameter and full length, for check weave
Finer rushes for three rod wale

Method

With the stakes, work a check weave base (see Rectangular Basket with Lid). Tie it firmly in place on the trough and, turning the stakes up the sides, work three rounds of three rod wale. Add an extra stake and, with the $\frac{1}{2}$ in. rushes, work five rounds of check weave. Using finer rushes, work three rounds of three rod wale and finish with Border 1.

51

Sampan

Materials
30 medium or fine rushes 24 in. in length, or long enough to cover the chosen mould
A small glass trough or sardine tin
A few finer rushes for pairing weave

Method
Start as for the Round Dinner Mat, making a square of check weave in the centre of the stakes. With the finer rushes, work two rounds of pairing weave.

Tie the square on to the glass trough, turning up fifteen ends front and back. Join these together at the top with two rows of pairing weave and fasten off the two weavers neatly. Trim the ends of the stakes to within an inch of the rows of pairing weave. Take the fifteen ends on the right and bind them together near the ends with a strong rush. Do the same with those on the left. Set them into a boat shape and trim close to the binding rush. Allow to dry.

The Sampan is quickly made, and effective as a table decoration. It can be used with a cargo of toys or sweets as a party centrepiece, or filled with eggs and chicks at Easter.

MOBILES

Ship mobile

Materials

2 willow wands 12 in. in length
Smaller and thinner pieces for masts
A few fine rushes
4 thick rushes for plaiting
3-ply seaming string and a sailmaker's needle
A sharp penknife

Method

Using the penknife make a slit in the centre
of one of the pieces of willow and pass the
other piece through it at right angles. With
a long piece of string tie the willow wands
together at the centre so that they balance
on the end of the string. Cover them neatly
with a round plait made with the four thick
rushes, but starting with only two bent
double over the end of the willow to give
four ends for the plait. Finish neatly.

Take a dozen 7 in. lengths of rush and,
making them into two groups, stitch them
together using the same stitch as for the Ali
Baba Linen Basket. String or a fine rush may
be used for the stitching. Shape the boat and
stitch a similar group of six rushes to each
side. Bind the ends tightly and trim close.
Set in a good shape and allow to dry.

From the thin willow twig cut a piece 4
in. in length, trim to a point at one end and
insert it in the boat to make a mast. Make a
small slit at the top of the mast. To make the
sail, take about a dozen smooth round pieces
of rush and, placing them horizontally across
the mast, thread them together up the right-
hand side with fine thread. Take the thread
through the slit in the top of the mast and
through the rushes on the other side of the
sail. Stitch the thread into the bottom of the
boat at both sides. Trim the rushes neatly.
Make three more ships in the same way.

52

Attach the ships to the frame with black thread, letting them hang about 4 in. down. Threads may be taken from the bound ends of the boat via the mast and upwards to the frame to make the ships balance.

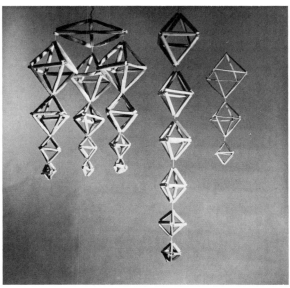

53

Openwork mobiles

Materials

A quantity of short lengths of rush (pieces trimmed from finished baskets or mats are suitable)
A long darning needle
A ball of soft white embroidery cotton
A bundle of fine green florist's wire

Method

Wet the short pieces of rush and allow them to dry without letting them touch each other. They should be round and smooth to get the best effect.

For the triple mobile, cut twelve pieces of matching rush 3½ in. in length. Thread the darning needle with 1½ yards of the soft cotton and push it down the centre of one of the rushes. Add two more (as if threading beads) and push them gently to within 2 or 3 in. of the other end. Tie these rushes into a triangle and thread two more. Half hitch these with the needle on to the thread of the first triangle (in either corner away from the tie) and thread two more rushes. Half hitch these on to the previous two (between the two) and thread two more. Continue in this way until five triangles have been made. Thread the last rush and tie to the beginning thread. Trim one end of this tie away. Take a short thread and tie the two outside angles of the series of five triangles together and trim the ends of the string close.

Make a second section with pieces of rush $2\frac{1}{2}$ in. long, a third with pieces $1\frac{1}{2}$ in. long and a fourth with pieces $\frac{3}{4}$ in. long. Tie all the sections together with half an inch of single thread between each, and the first drop is complete. Make two more drops.

To make the frame, take three pieces of rush 7 in. in length and, threading the florist's wire through them lengthwise, make a complete triangle. Take three pieces of rush 5 in. in length and, threading a length of wire through each, join one to each corner of the triangle and then join the three loose ends together and make a loop to hang the mobile. Hang it on a fairly long string and it will turn gently. Hang the three drops from it, leaving one inch of thread between the frame and the first drop.

The long single mobile is made in a similar way using lengths of rush $3\frac{1}{2}$ in., 3 in., $2\frac{1}{2}$ in., 2 in., $1\frac{1}{2}$ in. and 1 in. for the different sections.

The short single mobile is made with fine rushes using lengths of $3\frac{1}{2}$ in., $2\frac{1}{2}$ in. and $1\frac{1}{2}$ in. for different sections.

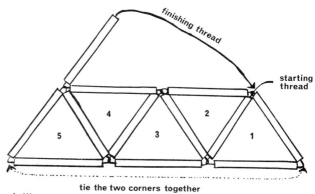

xlviii

tie the two corners together

73

54

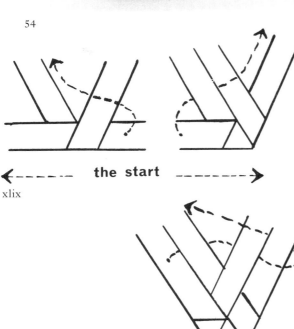

the start

l

the plait

TABLE LAMPS

Table lamp in diagonal weave

Materials

A small wooden or plastic bowl
The inner tube of a kitchen roll
About 30 rushes $\frac{1}{2}$ in. in diameter, for stakes
Medium rushes for weaving
A buckram lampshade

Method

Make a hole in the centre of the base of the bowl. To determine the necessary length for the stakes, measure round the outside of the bowl from rim to rim and add 16 in. for the border. Cover the bowl, starting with a check weave centre (the one illustrated is $5'' \times 5''$ stakes) and adding extra stakes in the corners as for the Square Dinner Mat. Tie the base on to the bowl and change to diagonal pairing weave, making sure that the total number of stakes is divisible by four and adding an extra stake to make the odd number required for the pattern. Continue to the top of the bowl and finish with Border 4.

Cover the tube in the same weave, then turn the bowl upside down to make a base for the column. Fill the column with cotton reels and thread the electric cable through them and through the hole in the bowl. Join base and column securely together.

Make a criss-cross pattern round the shade with flattened pieces of rush and attach them with a transparent adhesive. Make a flat folded plait as shown in diagrams xlix and l (working upwards).

Continue with the same movement from each side in turn until the plait is of sufficient length to go round the top and bottom of the shade. Attach with adhesive, finishing neatly.

Covered wine bottle with shade

Materials
20 rushes $\frac{1}{2}$ in. in diameter, for stakes
Finer rushes for pairing weave
A hock bottle with the label removed
A buckram shade

Method
Tie the twenty rushes together 3 in. from the butt end and slip the base of the bottle into the long rushes as near to the knot as possible. Take fine weavers and work in pairing weave for an inch or so until the bottle is firmly held in the rushes. Turn the bottle round, and with the neck facing, start a round of knots.

55

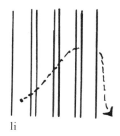
li

lii

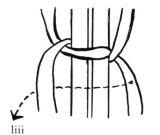
liii

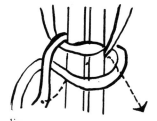
liv

This is a reef knot over two rushes. Work the next round in the same way, but taking two rushes from each knot.

Work in this way till the shoulder of the bottle is reached. Turn the bottle the right way up and change to pairing weave. As the neck of the bottle narrows, take two rushes

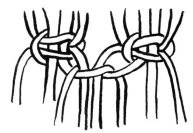
lv

together occasionally and reduce the number of stakes to ten. Finish with Border 4 and trim below the double plait. Turn the bottle upside down, untie the knot and, damping the stakes, finish with Border 4 round the base of the bottle.

The shade in the illustration is made from buckram trimmed with textured wool and single rushes. The braid is a ZIG-ZAG PLAIT made with a single rush held in place in the centre with a row of pairing weave.

Twist the rush round itself as shown and work the row of pairing weave between each twist to give the effect illustrated.

lvi

WALL HANGINGS

Sunflower wall hanging

Materials

A piece of insulation board about 24″ × 36″
About 130 rushes ½ in. in diameter for covering the board
A few very thick rushes for the sunflowers
A quantity of rush flower heads with 12 in. stalks attached
A few fine rushes for pairing weave
Two or three rods to prevent the warp from getting too tight

Method

Place a series of rushes side by side across the board, tying each in a reef knot at the back, making a rush warp. It is advisable to take them over two or three rods placed at intervals on the right side to ensure that the warp is not too tight (these are removed as the weaving proceeds). Use the remainder of the rushes to complete the cover by weaving under and over the warp in a manner similar to check weave. The warp should be close, but the weft may be a little more open.

Make about four yards of FOLDED TWO-PLAIT by bending a rush at right angles, folding the two ends over alternately and pressing between the fingers and thumb of the left hand.

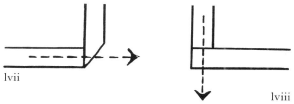

lvii   lviii

This plait should be worked upwards and produces a concertina effect. Arrange the plait on the covered board as shown in diagram lix.

56

lix

77

Make the sunflowers in various sizes in zig-zag plait (see lampshade for Covered Wine Bottle) joining the plait into a ring with one or two rounds of pairing weave. Arrange them on the board.

Take the flower heads and, working close to the heads, join them together in twos with a row of pairing weave, finishing neatly. Cross the double stakes (as for Openwork Basket 1) and with two new weavers work a row of pairing about an inch above the first. Cross the stakes again and with new weavers work two or three rows of close pairing weave and finish with Border 1. Attach the fringe to the bottom of the wall hanging.

Small wall hanging in check weave

Materials
A piece of hardboard 20″ × 5″
About 60 rushes ½ in. in diameter
2 rods 6 in. in length for the top and bottom of the hanging
2 longer rods to prevent the warp from getting too tight

Method
Place the short rods at the top and bottom of the board and make a warp by tying ten rushes round the board, inserting the longer rods at the same time. Work in check weave from the bottom to the top of the board, removing the long rods in the process. Make a fine rope across the top rod for hanging.

Make a MONKEY'S FIST KNOT by taking a strong rush, holding the starting end under the left thumb and winding
3 times round the hand (all four fingers together)
3 times round the middle of the hank
3 times through the loops of the first hank (by threading the working end).

start

finish

1x

57

Work the knot tight, cut off both ends and slip the knot on to the end of one of the short rods. Make three more knots in the same way for the other ends. This hanging is intended for arrangements of fresh flowers and saves precious space in small rooms.

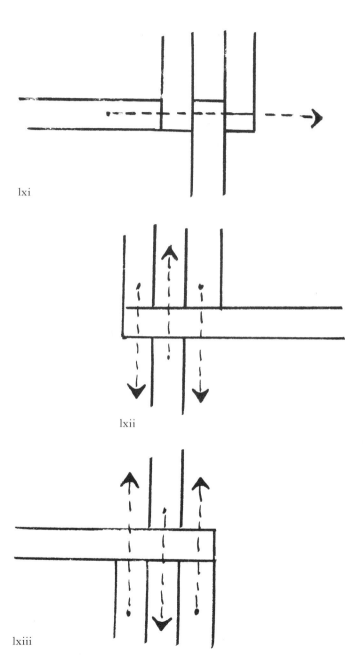

lxi

Wall hanging on black cotton satin background

Materials
A piece of thick cardboard 24″ × 7″, covered with black cotton satin and finished with 9 in. rods at top and bottom
About 25 rushes ½ in. in diameter

Method
Double two rushes, tie them to a hook in the wall and, using the four ends, make 6½ in. of round plait. Untie the string and arrange the rushes at the working end of the plait as shown in diagram lxi.

Fold the single rush over the other three, and fold the three rushes over the single rush in the directions indicated.

lxii

Bring the single rush back over the other three and fold the three rushes back over it.

This plait should be pressed firmly between the fingers and thumb of the left hand and will give a concertina effect. When the desired length is reached, tie one rush round the other three and trim, leaving some 2 in. at the end of the plait.
    Double three rushes and using the six ends make 10 in. of round plait. Change to a

lxiii

79

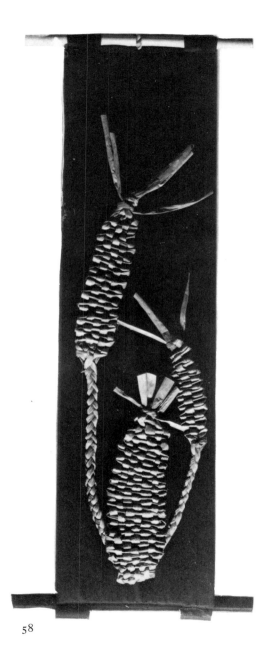

folded five-plait over one rush, worked in the same way as the plait described above. Make a folded seven-plait over one rush for the centre. Tie the ends and trim, leaving an inch or so of plain rush. Arrange the plaits on the background as shown, and attach with transparent adhesive.

With fine rushes, make a rope loop to hang the panel.

This panel was made as a teaching aid to show the development of round plaits into textured plaits.

58

59–61 Other suggested arrangements for wall panels using decorative plaits.

59

60

61

NAPKIN RINGS

Napkin ring in pairing weave (see frontispiece)

Materials

A cylindrical mould with a circumference of about 7 in. (the ring illustrated was made round a 4 oz cream jar)
7 rushes $\frac{1}{2}$ in. in diameter and 12 in. in length
A few finer rushes for pairing weave

Method

Working on the table, bend one stake double and start pairing weave on the second half.

Add another bent stake and pair over both halves. Continue in this way until all stakes are used. Place them round the mould and join into a ring by pairing over the first half of the first stake. Work in neat pairing weave for six or seven rounds, damp the stakes and finish with Border 1.

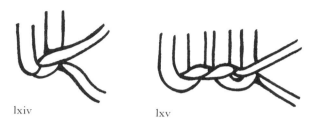

lxiv   lxv

62

Turk's head napkin ring

Make two yards of fine three-plait and wind it tightly round the four fingers of the left hand as shown in diagram lxvi.

Pass the right-hand loop A under B and carry the working end to the left over B and under A. Bring it down the back of the hand to the start. This completes the first round and the pattern should be distributed evenly round the ring. The strands may then be doubled or trebled by weaving under and over in the same pattern with the working end.

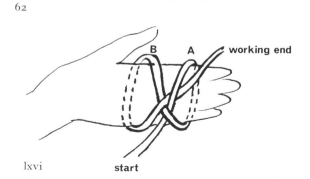

lxvi   start

63

SECTION VI
Toys

Horses

Materials

38 in. of $\frac{3}{4}$ in. three-plait
3-ply seaming string and a sailmaker's needle

Method

Cut two lengths of plait, each about 11 in. long, bind the ends with string and trim close. Bend them into a curve for the body and feet (diagram lxvii). Bind one end of the remaining piece of plait. To make the head, bend back just over an inch of the bound end, and bringing the plait round the bound end and up again, stitch the three thicknesses together. Blind-stitch down the neck and stitch this length between the other two for about 3 in. Bind the end of the centre plait after undoing the last few inches to make a tail. Draw a rush through the top of the head to make two ears and bind the nose tightly with string.

The small horse stands on figure-of-eight knots which are made at the ends of the plaits, and longer pieces of plait will therefore be required for the legs. For the FIGURE-OF-EIGHT-KNOT, make a loop B and bring the working end round behind A, over B and down through the loop.

Tighten the knot and trim the ends. This gives a round knot for the feet.

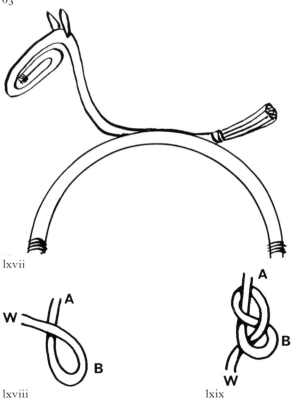

lxvii

lxviii   lxix

Rush rattle

Materials

7 fine, but strong and pliable rushes
A small bell
A rug needle

Method

Tie the rushes together 6 in. from the butt and tie again at the butts. This length is used as a core and the rattle is worked round it. Spread out the rushes and picking up one rush (A), take it over B and C in an anti-clockwise direction.

Pick up C and A together and, giving both a sharp twist to the right, carry C over D, leaving A behind. Twist C and D to the right and take D over E. Continue in this way, working outwards from the core for about six rounds to allow room for the bell. Work straight for three rounds, place the bell in position and begin to draw in towards the handle, which is worked very tightly round the core of seven butts.

When the handle is long enough, trim off the butts forming the core and work on without a core to make a loop at the end of the handle. When this part of the plait is about 2 in. long, bend it round to the end of the handle and, with a rug needle, weave the seven ends away into the plait in pattern.

If it is necessary to join in the course of the plaiting, push the pith out of the way with a fine skewer and insert the new rush.

The rattle shown in the centre of photograph 64 is finished with a simple three-plait handle.

64

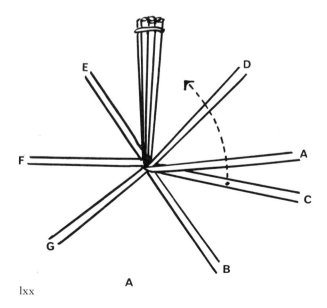

lxx

85

Child's basket

Materials

A small round mould in plastic or tin (the basket illustrated was made on a container $2\frac{1}{2}$ in. in diameter and $1\frac{3}{8}$ in. in depth)
12 rushes rather less than $\frac{1}{2}$ in. in diameter, and 12 in. in length
Very fine rushes for pairing weave

Method

Using the rushes six by six, make a centre of check weave and tie it on to the mould. Work in pairing weave, undoing the corners of the check weave to make a round shape, and arranging the stakes so that they are evenly spaced. Continue up the sides in fine pairing weave to the top of the basket.

BORDER 6 (three rod plain in two rounds). Twist the first stake and pass it behind the second, leaving the projecting end outwards to the right.

Twist the second stake behind the third and continue in this way until the final stake is threaded through the loop of the first stake. Twist one of the projecting rushes and, using the awl, pass it over two stakes and through the next loop, then bring the end to the outside of the basket under the border.

Continue in this way until the border is complete.

On a large strong basket it is desirable to carry the ends under the last four rounds of pairing weave, but on the small basket illustrated the ends are trimmed in the traditional manner, i.e., leaving half an inch of the stake projecting.

This basket may also be used for miniature flower arrangements. The two baskets in the front of photograph 65 are made from grass by the same method as the Ali Baba Linen Basket.

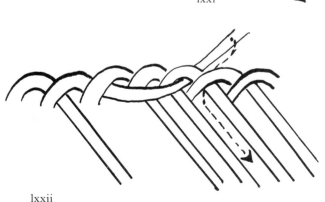

lxxi

lxxii

86

Flower basket over an egg-cup

Materials

An egg-cup
6 rushes $\frac{1}{4}$ in. in diameter and 12 in. in length
A few very fine rushes for pairing weave

Method

Using the 12 in. rushes three by three, make a check weave centre and tie it on to the egg-cup. Work in fine pairing weave up the sides of the egg-cup, adding extra stakes if necessary. When the top of the egg-cup is reached, turn it upside down on the table with stakes spread out around it. Work on these for an inch or so and finish with Border 1.

Turn the flat weaving up at the back and down at the front of the egg-cup. Make a long plaited handle and attach it to the back and front of the basket.

66

Easter table decoration

Materials

About 3 yards plaited leaves (e.g., iris or montbretia)
3-ply seaming string
A sailmaker's needle and sailor's palm

Method

Make a small basket in the same way as the Plaited Bowl. The basket in the illustration is filled with small Easter eggs and covered with a papier-mâché sitting hen. This is made from old magazine paper, shaped in the hand and painted with poster colours. It gives great delight to children and the cost is negligible.

Rushes (*about 5 lb to a bolt*)	Tom Metcalfe Arnold Holywell St Ives Huntingdon
	Dryad Handicrafts Limited Northgate Leicester (Large orders only)
	Nottingham Handicraft Company Melton Road West Bridgford Nottingham (Large orders only)
	Jacobs, Young and Westbury Bridge Road Haywards Heath Sussex
	Debenham Rush Weavers Debenham Suffolk
	Gray and Cahill 122 Peckham Road London SE5
Seaming string *Sailmaker's needle* *Sailor's palm*	William Good and Son 46 Fish Street Hill London, EC3
Stool frames *Frame for garden trug*	Craft shops and do-it-yourself shops
Football lacing awl	Obtainable from any sports shop

Rushes

Alnap Company Inc.
66 Reade
New York, N.Y. 10007

S & S Arts and Crafts
Norwich Avenue
Colchester
Connecticut 06415

National Handicrafts Company
225 Lafayette
New York, N.Y. 10012

Seaming string

Di Mattina Supply Company
59 Seabring
Brooklyn N.Y. 01231